CONTENTS

1. What do we mean by food matters? 7

2. How does diet affect health? 15

3. Why do people diet? 21

4. What are eating disorders? 25

5. Why are some people vegetarians? 29

6. What are food allergies? 35

7. What is food poisoning? 41

8. Do we need intensive farming? 47

9. How is science changing our food? 53

   Helplines 59

   Further reading 60

   Index 61

FOOD MATTERS

JILLIAN POWELL

EVANS BROTHERS LIMITED

Evans Brothers Limited
2A Portman Mansions
Chiltern Street
London W1M 1LE

First published 1998

British Library Cataloguing in Publication Data.

Powell, Jillian
    Food matters. - (Life Files)
    1.Food - Juvenile literature
    I.Title
    641.3

ISBN 0 237 51811 2 (hardback)

ACKNOWLEDGEMENTS

Editorial: Su Swallow
Design: Tinstar Design
Production: Jenny Mulvanny

For permission to reproduce copyright material the
Author and Publishers gratefully acknowledge the
following: **cover** Mark Segal/Getty Images
page 7 (top) Food Features (bottom) Donna Day/Getty
Images **page 9** Laurence Monneret/Getty Images
page 11 Adina Tovy/Robert Harding Picture Library
page 12 Mike Blank/Getty Images **page 16**
Vanderharst/Robert Harding Picture Library **page 17**
David Lansdown/Sylvia Cordaiy Photo Library **page
18** David Cumming/Eye Ubiquitous **page 19** Robert
Harding Picture Library **page 21** Paul Seheult/Eye
Ubiquitous **page 23** Lori Adamski Peek/Getty Images
page 25 Robert Harding Picture Library **page 26** Dale
Durfee/Getty Images **page 28** Image Bank **page 29**
Chris Bayley/Getty Images **page 31** Robert Harding
Picture Library **page 33** Paul Seheult/Eye Ubiquitous
page 34 Raphael Buchler/Getty Images **page 35** Mark
Azavedo Photo Library **page 36** Yiorgos Nikiteas/Eye
Ubiquitous **page 37** Robert Harding Picture Library
page 39 Chris Parker/Sylvia Cordaiy Photo Library
page 41 Michael Rosenfeld/Getty Images **page 42**
Food Features **page 43** Robert Harding Picture Library
page 44 E. Simanor/Robert Harding Picture Library
page 47 L. Johnstone/Eye Ubiquitous **page 48** Paul
Seheult/Eye Ubiquitous **page 53** Robert Harding
Picture Library **page 54** Gavin Wickham/Eye
Ubiquitous **page 56** Mark Segal/Getty Images

WHAT DO WE MEAN BY FOOD MATTERS?

Food is important in all our lives. We need food to live, to grow and to stay healthy. Food is part of our lifestyle. Eating can be a rushed snack in front of the television, or a social occasion with friends. Food is used to celebrate events such as birthdays, marriages, and religious festivals. Eating habits are often formed when we are children, and can affect our health as we grow older. Today, the supermarket culture means that a wider variety of foods is available to us all year round than ever before. But in recent years a number of food scares have cast doubt on the safety and quality of our food. Many people are questioning the way food is produced and processed today. Issues such as food safety, additives, irradiation, animal welfare and genetic engineering have made food into regular headline news.

Top right: The food habits we form as children can affect our health for the rest of our lives.

Right: The diet we eat and the amount of exercise we take are the main ways we have of taking care of our health.

WHAT DO WE MEAN BY DIET?

Diet is the food a person usually eats every day. There are also special diets such as slimming diets, vegetarian diets and low fat diets. Many factors influence the diet we choose. They include the cost and availability of food, advertising and labelling, our lifestyle, ethnic traditions and religion.

> **"The energy saved by inactive living can be very substantial and will ultimately be laid down as fat. Normal people have been ambushed by the insidious effects of modern sedentary life. They don't mean to get fat and unhealthy, life has just changed without them noticing it."**
>
> Dr Andrew Prentice, Dunn Clinical Nutrition Centre, Cambridge, October 1997

Question
How balanced is your daily and weekly diet?

DIET IN HISTORY

The human diet has changed and evolved throughout history. Early peoples were hunter-gatherers. They spent their days searching for food and water, picking wild fruits and berries, digging up roots, and eating animals and fish they had trapped and hunted. They lived in small groups and moved around, following animals and seasonal changes in vegetation. By about 10,000 BC, people in the area now called the Middle East began to settle and practise agriculture. They learned to tame and breed animals, sow, plough and fertilise the land, and improve crops by selecting the best grain for the next year. Settled agriculture brought larger and more regular food supplies, although crops could still be lost because of climate or pests, and at the end of each winter, food became scarce.

Nomadic tribes, conquering armies and traders helped to carry foods to different parts of the world. The Arabs brought citrus fruits, rice and sugar to Europe in the Middle Ages. Later, Europeans spread foods such as maize from the Americas around the world. In the nineteenth century, the variety of foods available expanded due to new technology such as canning and freezing, and faster transport by rail and sea. New machinery meant that foods such as refined flour and milled rice, previously only available to the rich, went into mass production. Some processes resulted in nutritional losses. When polished white rice replaced unmilled brown rice in Asia in the late nineteenth century, the deficiency disease beriberi became widespread. This led to research into the nutritional content of rice germ, and the discovery of the importance of vitamins in the diet.

> 66 **Importing fresh fruit and vegetables into the UK is essential if we are to provide consumers with what they want: a wide selection and steady supply of fresh produce. Without them, the nation's diet would suffer, especially that of the growing number of vegetarians.** 99
>
> Ron Parker, Chairman of the Fresh Fruit and Vegetables Information Bureau

NUTRITION

Food is made up of chemical compounds called nutrients. They include proteins, carbohydrates, fats, vitamins and minerals. Different foods contain different amounts of nutrients. The body needs enough of each nutrient to grow, have energy, and fight diseases. All nutrients are important for our well-being, but we need them in different amounts. For example, we need about 250 grams of carbohydrates a day, but less than two micrograms of vitamin B12. A deficiency of any nutrient weakens the body and slows down cell growth and renewal.

When we eat, our digestive systems process food, using chemicals and acids to break it down so that nutrients can pass into the bloodstream and be carried round the body.

- **Carbohydrates** break down to glucose to provide energy.

- **Proteins** break down to amino acids which build and repair body cells.

- **Fats** break down to fatty acids which give warmth and can be stored as energy.

- **Vitamins and minerals** break down to keep different body cells healthy. Vitamin C, for example, helps us fight off illnesses, and keeps skin and blood healthy. Vitamin D helps build healthy teeth and bones.

A balanced diet means a diet that provides the correct amount of nutrients for an individual's needs. Nutritionists give guidelines on the amount of nutrients we need daily from our food but they depend on our sex, age, health, body build and lifestyle. Some groups, like babies, pregnant women, the sick and the elderly, have special dietary needs.

In pregnancy, women need to eat plenty of fresh fruit and vegetables, as well as taking supplements like folic acid.

> Many of us worry about our weight, so we tend to know something about diet, which may be defined as our daily intake of food and drink. Nutrition is a broader concept, embracing all the processes involved in using foodstuffs for the body's growth, maintenance and repair. As such, it is of vast importance to our health, yet we do not know much about it.
>
> Dr H.E. Stanton, in *The Healing Factor*

No single food provides all the nutrients we need. To have a balanced diet, we need to choose foods from each of four main food groups daily. We can supplement the diet with occasional foods from group five.

The four main food groups are:

1 Starchy carbohydrates eg bread, pasta, rice, cereals, potatoes, maize.

These should form the main part of each meal. They provide carbohydrates, B vitamins, some protein and minerals.

2 Meat and alternatives eg meat, fish, cheese, pulses, eggs, nuts.

These are high protein foods. They also provide some fat, B vitamins and minerals.

3 Dairy foods eg milk, cheese, yoghurt.

These provide protein, fats, vitamins A and D and the mineral calcium, needed for healthy teeth and bones.

4 Vegetables and fruit eg salads, fruits, leafy vegetables.

These are high in vitamins and minerals.

5 Sugary and fatty foods eg cakes, biscuits, sweets, crisps.

These should only be eaten occasionally and should not replace foods from the main four groups. They provide fats and sugars.

We also need water and non-starch polysaccharides (fibre). Water carries the nutrients from digested food into the bloodstream and passes waste out of the body as urine. Nonstarch polysaccharides are found in plant foods such as pulses, brown rice and pasta, wholemeal bread, fruit and vegetables. They keep the digestive system working properly, enabling us to digest food and pass solid waste.

When we eat food, our body converts it into energy. This is measured in units called kilocalories. About half the calories we take in are used for activity. The rest are used for growing, breathing and body processes such as digestion. If we take in more calories than we are using up through activity, our body stores the excess as fat.

A HEALTHY DIET

In recent years, there have been numerous studies into healthy eating. Most nutritionists are now agreed that we should eat more starchy carbohydrates and double our intake of vegetables and fruit to 400 grams or five portions a day. They recommend eating a wide variety of foods, fresh rather than processed, and maintaining a healthy body weight. They also advise limiting amounts of fat and sugar in the diet.

We need some fats in the diet, but most people eat more than they need. It is especially important to cut down on saturated fats, found mainly in animal products like meat, milk and cheese. Sugar contains no useful nutrients. If we eat too much it can be stored as fat and lead to weight problems. It is also the main cause of tooth decay. Advice to limit the amount of salt and alcohol in the diet is also based on studies linking these with health problems.

These are some of the recommendations for making our diet healthier:

- Change our eating patterns to conform to current health guidelines.

- Ask for healthy options in supermarkets, restaurants and cafés.

- Contact the local health education unit and dietetic department for advice on nutrition.

- Find out if the local education authority has a healthy eating policy.

- Write to the local MP on issues such as healthy school meals and additives.

Question
Does your local education authority have a healthy eating policy?

Fast foods like burgers and milkshakes, which can be high in fat and sugar, have become part of our lifestyle.

CHANGES IN DIET AND EATING HABITS

Changes in our diet in the last 50 years reflect wider social, economic and cultural changes. In the developed world the average family has got smaller, and their wealth has increased, bringing widespread ownership of freezers, microwaves and other appliances. Families no longer always eat together. A 1993 market research survey found that only 50 per cent of families sit down to eat together each evening. Over a third of families eat meals in front of the television. There has also been an increase in snacking and 'grazing' – eating in small quantities throughout the day.

Food technology has created a wide range of processed and ready meals. Around 75 per cent of the average diet today is processed foods. More meals are eaten outside the home and as takeaways, from fast food outlets. Changes in the way we buy our food mean that the major supermarkets now have 70 per cent of the grocery trade. The supermarket culture has enabled a wide range of fresh foods to be available at competitive prices. This has put pressure on farmers and growers to maintain continuous, stable supplies and consistent quality. Seasonal changes in foods have disappeared as more food is imported and scientists extend animal breeding seasons and new crop varieties that can be harvested through the year.

Fast food restaurants like this Tokyo diner are popular all over the world.

> For decades now, even a century, we have given food insufficient status. We have only been interested in cheap food, and we want to shop as fast as possible, cook as fast as possible and eat as fast as possible. What are the two things that Britain spends more on per head of the population than any other country? Videos and microwave cookers. That says such a lot about what has happened to our society, a culture that is tv-dominated and puts convenience, speed and price above quality, desirability and enjoyment.
>
> Professor Richard Lacey, Head of Clinical Microbiology at Leeds University

A century ago, most food was produced and sold locally. Now, the food chain extends from farmers, through processors, packers and hauliers to retailers and consumers. Food miles are the distance food travels from the point of origin to sale. In the US, food travels an average 1100 food miles, and in Europe, the contents of the average shopping trolley have travelled 2200 food miles. Some people believe this is an unnecessary waste of resources. Recently, there have been initiatives by some major supermarkets to bring more locally grown foods on to their shelves.

> The development of transport and the food chain has made it possible to import fruit and vegetables from the far corners of the world in record time. But the number of food miles involved in transporting produce over long distances has hidden costs, taking an environmental toll both in terms of the resources used and pollution produced.
>
> Nick Watts, Lincolnshire farmer

DIET AROUND THE WORLD

Modern methods of storage and transport carry a wide variety of foods around the world, but the diet we eat still depends on where we live. Around 800 million people, mostly living in developing countries, don't get enough to eat and suffer from malnutrition. Many of the rest eat too much and suffer from obesity and diet-related diseases. The rich, industrialised parts of the world produce and consume the most food, and have the smallest populations. The poor, developing parts of the world have the least food and highest populations.

In rich countries, farming and food production are highly mechanised. Technological advances have enabled high yields, creating surpluses of food. Thirty-seven per cent of plant foods produced are used to feed animals to produce meat and dairy foods. In poorer, developing countries, plant foods like rice and maize are the staple foods. The diet people eat is affected by crop failures, poor climate, wars and unstable economic conditions. Large areas of land may be used to grow cash crops like sugar and bananas for export, rather than growing food for the people. The farmers often receive only a fraction of the price paid for the food by consumers, so remain caught in the poverty trap. Some organisations like Traidcraft are now buying products such as sugar, tea and coffee direct from farmers or communities in developing countries to ensure that the producers receive a fair price. Fair trade is one of many issues surrounding the food we eat today.

Find out!

Which foods in your local supermarket do you think have travelled the most food miles? Find out if it stocks any local produce.

HOW DOES DIET AFFECT HEALTH?

There is increasing evidence that diet is an important factor in many diseases, including coronary heart disease, about a third of all cancers, non-insulin dependent diabetes, obesity, gallstones and dental decay.

Research into the links between diet and disease began in the early 20th century. Soldiers fighting in the First World War (1914 - 18) were found to have scurvy due to vitamin C deficiency. By the start of the Second World War (1939 - 45) the UK government had established the basic nutritional requirements for growth and health on which rationing was based. Many people ate more healthily during the war because the diet was rich in starchy carbohydrates but restricted meat, fats and sugars.

In recent years, there have been many studies into the links between diet and disease. These reports are often controversial, because health is affected by other factors, including family history, lifestyle and smoking. Nevertheless, it is estimated that around 50,000 people in the UK develop cancer each year because of unhealthy eating habits. The UK also has one of the highest rates of heart disease in the world. The British Heart Foundation has recently found signs of heart disease in children as young as seven. Coronary heart disease and some cancers have been linked with intake of fats, especially saturated fats,

in the diet. The average UK diet takes 40 per cent of energy from fats, while government recommendations advise a maximum of 35 per cent, of which only 10 per cent should be saturates, the rest polyunsaturated or monounsaturated fats. Saturated fats raise the level of a substance called cholesterol in the blood and cause the arteries to harden. This makes it more difficult for blood to flow easily and increases the risk of clots, leading to strokes and heart attacks. Too much salt in the diet is another risk factor. In the UK we eat about 10 grams of salt a day, mainly in processed foods, while the body needs only three grams.

THE MEDITERRANEAN DIET

Studies show that Mediterranean peoples eating a diet which is rich in plant foods but low in red meat and dairy products, have significantly lower levels of heart disease and cancer. The Mediterranean diet includes plenty of starchy carbohydrates such as bread, pasta, lentils and beans, as well as fresh fruit and vegetables, fish, olive oil and wine. Fresh fruit and vegetables, especially brightly coloured varieties, contain antioxidant vitamins which help the immune

Fruit and vegetables are rich in disease-fighting vitamins.

important part of Mediterranean dishes, as containing an anticancer and heart-disease chemical called lycopene.

Olive oil and wine may also be important factors in the diet. Olive oil is a monounsaturated fat which contains antioxidant vitamins and is believed to lower levels of blood cholesterol. Researchers have found grapes and red wine contain an anticancer substance called resveratrol, and wine is also believed to offer some protection against heart disease.

THE JAPANESE DIET

Breast cancer appears to be a western disease. The UK has the highest rate of death from breast cancer in the world, and women born and raised in the US are five times more likely to get breast cancer as women born and raised in Japan. If Japanese women emigrate to the West, however, they suffer the same rates as American and European women. This has led to scientific studies into the health benefits of the Japanese diet.

International comparisons show that breast cancer rates rise with fat consumption. The average rate of fat intake is lower in Japan than in Europe and the US. There is also scientific evidence to suggest that risk of breast cancer can be reduced by eating a diet high in soya products such as soy beans, miso, tofu and soya milk. Soy protein contains chemical compounds called isoflavanoids which appear to mimic the action of the breast cancer drug Tamoxifen. Like Tamoxifen, they may prevent the female

system to recognise and deal with potentially cancerous cells. The nonstarch polysaccharides (fibre) found in plant foods may also help reduce levels of cholesterol in the blood, and reduce some cancers and other diseases of the digestive system. Researchers from Columbia and Harvard Universities in the US single out tomatoes, an

hormone oestrogen from acting on the breast where it can trigger cancer.

People in Japan and China also have very low rates of colon and prostate cancer as well as coronary heart disease. Some studies suggest that fish oils protect against these diseases. They contain Omega 3 fatty acids which are believed to be anticancer agents as well as reducing levels of cholesterol in the blood. This evidence is supported by research into the diet of the Inuit people who consume high amounts of fatty animal and fish flesh, but have virtually no incidence of heart disease.

A steam boat is a traditional and healthy way of cooking in the East.

OBESITY

In the rich countries of the industrialised West, most diet-related diseases are caused by eating the wrong kinds of food, such as too many processed fatty and sugary foods, or by eating too much food, leading to obesity and related health problems. Obesity is a public health problem in all western countries, and is now increasing in developing countries like Jamaica. It can lead to the onset of non-insulin dependent diabetes, some cancers, coronary heart disease and gallstones.

In the UK, obesity has doubled in the last ten years, to 17 per cent of men and 13 per cent of women. Obesity in children is also a growing problem. A report by the National Forum for Coronary Heart Disease Prevention found 10 per cent of children in the UK to be overweight and nutritionists expect that figure to double by the year 2000. In the US, where Fat Camps for overweight children have become fashionable, one in four six-to-eleven year-olds is obese.

Medical experts estimate that most cases of obesity are caused by poor diet and lack of exercise. If we take in more energy than we use, the excess is stored as body fat. Many factors, such as cars, supermarket shopping, household gadgets and central heating in homes mean that people are less active than they used to be. Forty years ago, people ate between one quarter and one third more calories than they do today, but they did the equivalent of a marathon a week in extra physical activity. Research by the Dunn Clinical Nutrition Centre, Cambridge, found that today people use just 276 kcalories wheeling a trolley round a supermarket, compared with the 2400 kcalories used in the 1950s when they shopped by visiting

> ❝ The increase in grazing and snacking has increased the fat content of our diets. This, coupled with less exercise, means we are beginning to count the cost of these trends. ❞
>
> Dr Andrew Prentice, Head of Obesity Research, Dunn Clinical Nutrition Centre, Cambridge, 1997

Supermarkets have brought all our food shopping under one roof.

different shops in the high street. Children are also less active, spending more time watching television and using computers and less riding bicycles or doing outdoor games or sports. A child watching 28 hours of television a week, the UK average, uses nearly 600 calories a day less than children playing outdoors. Increasingly, children are driven to school rather than walking or cycling, and studies show that they eat over £220 million of sweets and snacks on the school run alone.

For each of us, there is a healthy weight range, appropriate to our height and body frame. We can calculate our Body Mass Index by dividing our weight in kilograms by our height in metres squared. A healthy BMI lies between 22 and 23. A BMI of over 30 is diagnosed as clinical obesity. Medical experts now agree that the health risks increase if the weight is carried around the waist (apple shape) as opposed to the hips and thighs (pear shape).

MALNUTRITION

There are already 5.5 billion people on the planet, and this figure is expected to rise to 10 billion by the year 2100. Food aid agencies currently estimate that every year 800 million people go hungry, and another 400 million consume less than 80 per cent of their basic food needs. Every year, up to 18 million people, mainly women and children, die of hunger. Most people who are undernourished live in the developing countries of Africa, Asia and Latin America.

Malnutrition means not taking in enough foods containing nutrients needed for health and growth. The diet in some developing

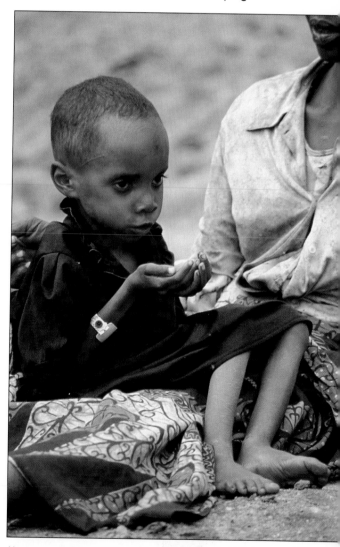

News reports bring pictures of starvation from developing countries like Rwanda. Malnutrition exists in developed countries, but receives less publicity.

countries can be very limited. In Sudan, for example, the daily diet consists of asida, a kind of porridge made from millet flour, supplemented with okra. Malnutrition can result in deficiency diseases such as beriberi, scurvy and rickets. In developed countries, people caught in the poverty trap may also be malnourished, due to a high intake of poor quality processed foods and low intake of important vitamins and minerals found in fresh foods such as fruit and vegetables.

Find out!
Half the sugar we eat is hidden in foods like ketchup, sausages and baked beans. Find out how much sugar there is in some of your favourite foods, and compare with any low sugar alternatives.

WHY DO PEOPLE DIET?

People diet for nutritional, health or cosmetic reasons. It is mostly women and girls who follow slimming diets. It is estimated that 95 per cent of women and girls diet at some point in their lives. Girls are showing awareness of body shape and dieting at an increasingly young age. One survey found that 41 per cent of nine-year-olds expressed the desire to be slimmer, and another recorded one in 10 six-year-olds as having dieted.

In the last 30 years, average height and weight have increased. At the same time, there has been increasing pressure to pursue a thin, even anorexic look. Magazines and advertisements promote images of underweight models like Kate Moss and Jodie Kidd. Watchmakers Omega recently withdrew advertisements from *Vogue* magazine in protest at the anorexic images being used. Today, the average model is thinner than 95 per cent of the rest of the population, and weighs nearly a quarter less

Media pressures have made children conscious of fashion ideals and turned many into dieters.

than the average woman. Fashion alters our perceptions. In the 1890s, young women read manuals on 'How to be Plump', but by the 1920s boyish shapes with slim hips and flat chests had become the ideal. Our cultural background also influences what we consider the ideal body shape. In many Polynesian societies, being plump is associated with having plenty, and is a sign of wealth and power.

> " Together with the media and fashion industry, the powerful diet food industry has artificially created a 'problem' which has resulted in the vast majority of women in Britain and other western developed countries feeling that they need to diet. "
>
> Mary Evans Young, *Journal of the National Consumer Council*, 1993

THE DIET INDUSTRY

The diet industry became big business in the late 1960s with the growth of self-help groups like Weight Watchers, health farms, slimming aids and remedies. Today the industry is worth over £1 billion in the UK alone. Recently, some MPs in the UK have called for stricter controls of 'miracle cure' products such as skin patches that claim to speed up the body's metabolic rate and sniffing sachets which claim to control chocolate addiction.

In recent years, slimming pills have begun to take a larger market share in the industry. Some are appetite suppressants. Others act as fat magnets, inhibiting the body's absorption of fats, or diuretics which strip the body of water and potassium. Appetite suppressants can lead to significant weight loss, but weight is easily regained when the drug is stopped. The health risks of slimming drugs include addiction, insomnia, depression, hair loss and even death. They are now widely seen as a last resort for cases of severe obesity, along with extreme methods like jaw wiring and gastric surgery.

DIET PLANS

Ideas about dieting change in line with research into nutrition and medicine. During the 1960s, calorie-counting and low carbohydrate diets were favoured. New research showing the importance of starchy carbohydrates and nonstarch polysaccharides (fibre) in the diet have now put the emphasis on a low-fat, high-fibre diet. Calorie-counting is still the most popular method of dieting, but nutritionists now advise a system based on balancing foods from the four main food groups (see page 10). Diets which are based on a single food type, such as exotic fruits, and diets based on low carbohydrate intake, such as the Scarsdale diet, are discouraged by medical experts.

> ❝ The culture created by advertising, the fashion world, the media and films glamorises an 'ideal' that is unhealthy, unnatural and uncomfortable to achieve. The diet industry arrogantly claims it always knows better than nature. It originated, and widely spreads, the all-pervading hysteria to the point that dieting has become part of life almost for its own sake. ❞
>
> Egon Ronay, *Egon Ronay Recommends*, 1994

Food-combining is a new version of the Hay diet pioneered in the I96Os. It is based on the principle that proteins and starches don't mix, so by avoiding combinations, food will be digested more efficiently and the body will lose weight. Some medical experts are sceptical, claiming that most foods combine both elements anyway.

An increasing trend is to put more emphasis on lifestyle and exercise, now recognised as important factors in losing weight.

Exercise is the fun way to burn calories and stay fit.

Many of the most popular diet plans take a themed approach, like the F Plan diet, which is based on the principle that eating more fibre prevents the body absorbing all the calories from food eaten. Medical experts generally approve the principle of a high-fibre, low-fat diet but some consider the levels of fibre in the diet to be too high.

Question
Why do you think 96 per cent of diets don't work?

Question
Scientists are experimenting with antifat injections on mice and pigs to find a solution to human obesity. Do you think this is the right way to tackle the problem?

HEALTH RISKS

Crash or starvation diets can bring sudden weight loss, but weight is usually rapidly regained. This is because dieting is now known to slow down the body's metabolic rate, making it hold on to fat stores more efficiently. Crash dieting carries health risks including heart stress, infertility and gallstones. Dieting can also lead to depression and mood swings by altering brain chemistry, and may trigger eating disorders. Weight-reducing diets carry particular risks for children as there is a danger of restricting height growth.

For adults, medical experts advise that slow, steady weight loss at the rate of 0.5-1 kg per week is best. For many people this will mean reducing their energy intake by about 1000 calories a day, but this will depend on their sex and age, how much weight they need to lose, and how active they are. A diet plan should be low in fat and sugar and high in starchy carbohydrates, fruit and vegetables, and include regular exercise.

DIET BREAKERS

The anti-diet movement was pioneered by psychotherapist Susie Orbach in the 1970s with her book *Fat is a Feminist Issue*. Organisations such as Diet Breakers, set up in 1992 by Mary Evans Young, have fuelled a new trend towards 'larger size acceptance'. Surveys by Dietbreakers show that 96 per cent of diets don't work. They hold counselling sessions to enable dieters to talk through their weight problems and diet obsessions. The aim is to help dieters develop a 'healthy relationship' with food again.

Question
How can 'larger size acceptance' be promoted?

WHAT ARE EATING DISORDERS?

Eating disorders can happen to anyone of any age, race or culture. Ninety per cent of sufferers are women and girls, but the number of men and boys with eating disorders is increasing. Eating disorders are about feelings, although they have physical effects on the body. They often develop as a way of coping with difficult or painful feelings. The eating disorder is an unconscious attempt to avoid those feelings and keep them under control.

Food is often tied in with our emotions.

> An eating disorder is not a sign that someone is greedy or inadequate or morally incomplete but usually a sign that something else is wrong. An eating disorder is often the only way people know how to cope.
>
> Deanne Jade, National Centre for Eating Disorders

We may all experience difficulties with eating at some time in our lives, but not all of us will go on to develop an eating disorder. Research has shown that some people may be genetically susceptible to developing an eating disorder. The personality of the

sufferer, and family relationships, may also be factors. The illness may be triggered by personal or family situations, such as bereavement, family breakup, bullying or abuse. Many sufferers believe they are to blame for something bad happening. They think of themselves as inadequate or worthless and use food to express their feelings about themselves. Food becomes the most important thing in their lives. A day is judged good or bad on how much food they have eaten or managed not to eat.

People are developing eating disorders at an increasingly young age. The Eating Disorders team at the Great Ormond Street Children's Hospital in London currently receives four referrals a week of children as young as seven with eating disorders. Some medical experts stress that the link between food and feelings begins in childhood. Children may be praised for eating up food. Food may be given as a comfort, and withholding food becomes a way of punishing the body. During adolescence, as bodies grow and develop, some start to feel self-conscious about putting on weight. Refusing food can also be part of the power struggle with parents. Dieting becomes a way of trying to gain control over at least one part of an adolescent's life: his or her body.

Images of slim, perfect bodies in advertisements and magazines create pressures to achieve impossible ideals. In her books *Fat is a Feminist Issue* and *Hunger Strike*, Susie Orbach has linked eating disorders to the changing role of women in society. Under increasing pressure to be successful at work and at home, many women feel their bodies are the one thing they can control. They become anorexic or bulimic, believing they can never match up to the ideals of the day. Compulsive eating and obesity may also be ways of protesting against society's slim sexual stereotypes.

The media bombard us with pictures of slim ideals.

ANOREXIA NERVOSA

Anorexia Nervosa was first recorded in the 19th century at a time when Victorian fashions stressed slim figures and tiny waists. Today it is increasingly common: an estimated one per cent of British women aged 14 to 23 years are anorexic. Anorexics are obsessed with their body weight and terrified of becoming fat. Their distorted body image means they see themselves as fat even when they are dangerously underweight. Girls may even avoid using handcream or toothpaste in case they add calories. They are afraid others will laugh at them or tease them if they eat normally and put on weight. Their lives revolve around avoiding eating, counting calories and exercising. They may be interested in cooking for others, but themselves skip meals, hide food and pretend they have eaten. Starving themselves and overexercising gives them a sense of achievement, but they then become depressed, tired and weak.

Like other eating disorders, Anorexia Nervosa is an isolating illness. A sufferer's family may think the sufferer is just going through a 'phase', or not realise what is happening until it is out of control. They may try to coax, force or trick the sufferer into eating. Rapid weight loss can make the sufferer irritable, angry and hostile. They may become so undernourished that they suffer from starvation symptoms such as stomach pains, dizziness, swollen legs and poor circulation. If puberty has started, periods may stop. Severe cases can damage the heart and brain, and cause brittle bones.

BULIMIA NERVOSA

Bulimia Nervosa typically begins during adolescence, mainly in girls, although sufferers may not seek help until they are in their 30s or 40s. Bulimia means 'eating like an ox'. Like anorexics (some of whom go on to develop Bulimia Nervosa), sufferers are obsessed with body weight and have a terror of becoming fat. They are often sensitive and self-critical and although they appear attractive and successful, inside they feel worthless and unloved. Bulimics binge eat, then make themselves sick or use laxatives to get rid of the food. They are often able to keep their illness secret as they maintain the same body weight. They hoard food, bingeing on ice cream, custard, cakes or chocolates, and even frozen or uncooked foods. They then feel ashamed and disgusted and punish themselves by vomiting or taking laxatives. They may also try crash-dieting and exercise a lot in an attempt to try and control their bodies.

> **By focussing their energies on controlling their bodies, they had found refuge from having to face the more painful issues at the centre of their lives.**
>
> Diana, the late Princess of Wales, speaking at a conference on Bulimia

Chronic bulimics may binge anything from 10 to 30 times a day. They can become moody, tearful and irritable and suffer from symptoms including sore throat and mouth ulcers, irregular periods, swollen glands, loss of hair and tooth decay caused by acid from being sick. In fact, vomiting only rids the body of 30 to 50 per cent of calories eaten. Laxatives strip the body of fluids not calories, and also remove essential minerals like potassium and sodium. Regular purging can upset the balance of nutrients in the body and prevent organs including the heart and kidneys from working properly.

COMPULSIVE OR BINGE EATING

Compulsive or binge eating disorder resembles Bulimia Nervosa except that sufferers don't purge to rid their bodies of food. Compulsive eaters binge on food even when they are full or not hungry. Eating becomes a way of comforting themselves or forgetting unhappy or difficult feelings. They are often afraid of food and feel panic about eating in public. In private, they lose control and binge on food, often cramming it in without tasting it. They feel out of control and may swing between bingeing then crash-dieting and exercising, in an attempt to regain control of their bodies. An estimated two per cent of the population suffer with binge eating disorder, and may become obese. Like other eating disorders, the illness makes sufferers tearful, moody and irritable.

TREATMENT

Although eating disorders can be serious and even life-threatening, early recognition and effective treatment is successful in most cases. But if the sufferer struggles on without help and support, the illness can develop into a chronic problem. There is much debate over the best methods of treatment for eating disorders. What works for one sufferer may not work for another. Most experts are agreed that while dietary monitoring and advice are important, treatment must also address the underlying psychological issues. It can take time to find the right kind of support and treatment. The first stage in getting help is for the sufferer to admit that there is a problem and that they need help.

> **66 Thinking about food becomes something you do almost all the time. All the energy you could be putting into other areas of your life goes into what you will and will not eat. That's why I went for help. I got so tired of getting up every single day thinking 'I want to eat but I can't.' 99**
>
> Liz Shepherd, *The Independent*, 1993

Treatment may need to involve the whole family. Sufferers' families often feel frightened of the illness and think they are being blamed by the professionals. People with an eating disorder may be concerned about how others will react, and afraid that their family and friends may no longer accept or love them. But talking about their illness can make them feel less isolated and being able to express how they feel is a key part of getting better. A doctor may suggest seeing a therapist or counsellor. Sufferers need to learn how to express their feelings clearly to others. They need to learn to care for their bodies and recognise that they don't have to be perfect. They also need to find ways of coping with their problems and with stress. Keeping a food diary can help them monitor

their behaviour and find out how their feelings affect what they eat. If a sufferer is severely underweight they may need to spend time in a special unit or hospital. Getting better can feel frightening. Sufferers may believe they don't deserve to get better and feel guilt or shame. They may suffer setbacks, especially at times of stress. It is important that they set realistic goals and don't try to rush recovery.

Keeping a food diary helps sufferers regain control.

Question
"Eating disorders are not primarily about eating or food." What do you think eating disorders are primarily about?

Find out!
Do your own research into the kind of images that the media use which influence our ideas about body shape. You could use magazines, newspapers, television and hoarding advertisements.

WHY ARE SOME PEOPLE VEGETARIANS?

Surveys show that a growing number of people are becoming vegetarian. Vegetarianism means eating a diet that avoids meat and foods made from animal products. Some vegetarians eat eggs and dairy products, others eat dairy products but no eggs. People who eat no meat, eggs or dairy products are vegans. The word vegetarian was first used in 1847 to describe the diet of people who set up the first Vegetarian Society in the UK. It comes from the Latin *vegetus*, which means lively.

In the last decade, the number of vegetarians in Britain has doubled to three million. A survey by the vegetarian food company Realeat in March 1997 found 5000 people a week converting to vegetarianism, especially among younger age groups. Current figures show 12 per cent of teenagers choose a vegetarian diet.

The vegetarian diet is based on four main food groups:

- **Cereals and grains**, eg bread, pasta, rice, cereals

- **Pulses, nuts and seeds**, eg baked beans, kidney beans, nuts, chickpeas, sunflower seeds

- **Fruit and vegetables**, eg broccoli, peppers, tomatoes, dried and fresh fruits

- **Soya and dairy products**, eg tofu, soya milk, TVP (textured vegetable protein) cow's milk, cheese, yoghurt

A vegetarian diet can provide all the nutrients we need, although like any diet it must be balanced, with foods chosen from the different food groups. It is important to eat a variety of protein foods such as beans, nuts or dairy products, to ensure the body takes in all the essential amino acids it needs.

Pasta and vegetables make a healthy, balanced vegetarian meal.

Plant foods can provide us with most of the vitamins and minerals we need. Vegans, who eat no eggs or dairy produce, can make sure they get vitamin Bl2 (only needed in tiny amounts) by eating Bl2-fortified foods.

MYTH
'Vegetarians don't get enough protein.'

FACT
Nutritionists now believe we take in far more protein than we need. This has been linked with osteoporosis and kidney disorders.

MYTH
'Vegetarians get anaemic through lack of iron.'

FACT
There is no evidence linking iron deficiency with a vegetarian diet. Iron is found in beans, lentils, green leafy vegetables and other plant-based foods.

MYTH
'Being vegetarian makes eating out difficult.'

FACT
More eating places are catering for vegetarians. A 1991 survey found 96 per cent of pubs offered vegetarian dishes.

People become vegetarian for different reasons. In developing countries, plant foods such as rice or wheat may be the only diet people can afford. Many others choose to be vegetarian for reasons of health, religious beliefs or because of their concern for animal welfare and the environment.

> **In the past, people were vegetarians because they disliked the killing of animals. The trend has now moved towards self interest. People feel healthier when they give up meat. They have more energy, sleep better and have less sinus trouble.**
>
> Greg Sams, *The Times*, November 1990

HEALTH BENEFITS

More people are becoming vegetarian for health reasons. A vegetarian diet is likely to be lower in fats, especially saturates, as fats in many plant foods are unsaturated. A 1995 report found that vegetarians have 30 per cent less likelihood of heart disease and 40 per cent less likelihood of cancer. Scientific evidence shows that high levels of antioxidants like betacarotene, and vitamins C and E, found in some fruits and vegetables, protect against some cancers and heart disease.

Recent meat scares such as BSE or mad cow disease, and food poisoning outbreaks caused by salmonella and E-coli bacteria have resulted in nearly half of the UK population eating less meat. Many people are also concerned about the use of antibiotics and hormones in meat production and additives such as nitrites, used as dyes and preservatives for bacon and ham. Some countries outside the European Union still use artificial hormones to boost growth, and antibiotics are used routinely as growth promoters as well as in veterinary treatment.

Recent studies in the United States have linked cancer with eating red meat. Some experts dispute this research, pointing out that US cancer rates may be influenced by the high amount of meat eaten and frequent barbecuing of meat, which has itself been linked with cancer. The UK government has issued guidelines advising consumers to cut down to less than 90 grams of red meat a day, and to increase levels of fresh fruit and vegetables in the diet.

> **Meat per se is not bad for you. You only have to look at the last remaining huntergatherers with a high meat diet, such as the Masai and the Bushmen of Southern Africa. They do not suffer from diseases associated with high meat diets of the West such as breast cancer and large bowel cancer. It is what farmers do to meat over here that is the problem. If animals were allowed adequate exercise and to eat grass and flowers as they did before the Second World War, then the fat content of meat would go down significantly.**
> Professor Michael Crawford, Director of the Institute of Brain Chemistry at Queen Elisabeth Hospital, *The Independent*, 1995

RELIGION

Many people are vegetarian because of religious beliefs. In India, 35 per cent of the population is vegetarian. Hindus believe that all life is sacred and that when someone dies their soul is born again into another person or animal. Strict Hindus avoid meat and fish, and all Hindus avoid eating beef because the cow is sacred in Hindu mythology. Many Sikhs are vegetarian and others avoid pork or beef. Buddhists believe it is wrong to kill or harm any living creature. Some are vegan and many others follow a vegetarian diet.

Indian markets provide a wide range of vegetarian foods.

ANIMAL WELFARE

> " In a lifetime, the average British meat-eater will consume 20 pigs, 29 sheep, five cattle and 760 poultry. "

Many people become vegetarian because they believe it is wrong to kill animals for food or because they believe the practices of modern factory farming are cruel. Most of the 700 million animals killed for food in the UK each year are raised on factory farms. Many animals are kept shut up in barren, crowded environments for their whole life, denying them their behavioural needs. Sows, which build nests for their young in the wild, give birth in narrow metal crates. Poultry, including chickens, turkeys and water fowl such as ducks, are kept in dimly lit sheds where the crowded conditions lead to symptoms of stress such as feather- and eye-pecking and even cannibalism. Animals and poultry bred for meat live only a few weeks of their natural lifespan, before enduring the stress of transport and slaughter.

Twenty million animals are sold every year at livestock markets. In the UK, market laws are controlled by MAFF's (The Ministry of Agriculture, Food and Fisheries) Codes of Practice, and enforced by local authority trading standards officers and veterinary surgeons. The Marketwatch scheme established by Animal Aid has highlighted many problems such as lack of water and lack of straw under foot, and frequent use of sticks to goad animals. Some people believe that live auctions should be replaced by electronic auctioneering, or animals sold direct to slaughterers or retailers to eliminate the stress caused by livestock markets.

Animals sold at market often face long journeys before slaughter. In the early 1990s, exports of live animals from the UK more than trebled, with over two million animals transported to the Continent on journeys of 40 hours or more often without food, water or rest. In the winter of 1994, violent clashes between animal welfare protestors and riot police focussed public attention on the issue of live exports. New European laws were introduced in 1996 to limit journey times to between 20 to 30 hours, with one-hour rests.

There is also concern that methods of slaughter are inhumane and can cause unnecessary suffering. By law, animals must be stunned before slaughter and remain so until dead, although animals killed ritually for Muslim or Jewish communities are exempted. In automated poultry slaughter, birds are hung upside down by their legs from a moving belt. Their heads pass through an electric water bath before their throats are cut, but some are not sufficiently stunned and they can even reach the scalding tank, for feather removal, while still alive. Welfare groups argue that these methods cause birds prolonged distress and there should be legislation to specify a minimum strength of electric currents.

1984, grain production per person has been falling. The production of protein in the form of meat, fish or soya is slowing down, but every year there are 91 million more human mouths to feed.

> **Nothing will benefit human health and increase chances for survival of life on Earth as much as the evolution to a vegetarian diet.**
>
> Albert Einstein, physicist and theorist (1879-1955)

As the human population goes on growing, it will be increasingly important to rely on vegetarian foods. Meat production is a wasteful way of using protein-rich crops. Only 10 per cent of the protein we feed to animals is turned into meat. Environmentalists argue that in land-use terms, a nonmeat diet is two to three times more efficient. Animal farming also requires more water.

> **It takes on average 13 litres of water to produce 500 grams of wheat, but 11,250 litres to produce the same amount of meat.**

Organisations such as the *RSPCA* and *Compassion in World Farming* have continued campaigning for Europe-wide legislation to limit journeys to a maximum of eight hours, with rules to ensure adequate food, water and rest.

ENVIRONMENTAL ISSUES

A 1993 survey by the Worldwatch Institute in Washington predicted that the world is entering an era of protein scarcity. Since

Factory farming is a major source of river and water pollution. Animal slurry leaks into rivers and streams, polluting and killing fish and other wildlife. Animals produce methane gases contributing to the greenhouse effect and global warming. Large areas of rainforest are cleared to make room for cattle ranching to produce meat for the burger trade. In South America, cattle ranching is responsible for up to half of rainforest destruction. Environmental groups also estimate that eight of the world's fishing grounds have been overfished and nine others are in danger. Stocks of fish have fallen so low that many countries have had to introduce quotas. Half the fish caught is used in animal feed or fertiliser.

Many people argue that vegetarianism offers the best solution for preventing a protein shortage in future and feeding the world's expanding population.

Question
Does your school or college offer vegetarian alternatives? If so, what percentage of people choose them?

Question
"It is fundamentally wrong and immoral to abuse and eat animals. We should make changes in our society to accommodate that moral principle." What kind of changes, if any, do you think need to be made?

Find out!
According to an NOP survey in June 1997, about 80 per cent of people want better welfare conditions for Britain's farm animals and seventy per cent are willing to pay more for a product from a humanely reared animal. Carry out your own survey at school to find out what people think.

Rainforests are cleared to supply meat for the burger trade.

WHAT ARE FOOD ALLERGIES?

Many people are intolerant of some foods in their diet. This means they have an unusual reaction to certain foods. Food intolerance can affect different parts of the body, causing skin rashes, eczema or asthma, arthritis, vomiting, diarrhoea, headaches and hyperactivity. Some reactions are mild, such as a skin rash or runny nose. Others are severe and life-threatening. There are no reliable figures for how many people are affected, but estimates suggest that between 10 and 25 per cent of the British population suffer from some form of food intolerance.

Food intolerance can have different triggers.

lack of a certain enzyme

Some people lack the enzymes that help them digest certain foods. For example, people with milk intolerance lack the enzyme lactase which helps us digest lactose, the natural sugar in milk.

histamine triggers

Foods such as strawberries can cause the release of a chemical called histamine in some people.

irritant effects

Highly spiced foods can cause irritation to the mouth and bowel.

pharmacological effects

Some substances, such as caffeine in coffee, can cause symptoms such as headaches, dizziness and sweating when taken in large amounts.

allergens

Some foods can cause an allergic reaction which involves the body's immune system.

Allergies to natural foods like strawberries may run in families.

FOOD ALLERGIES

Food allergy is a form of food intolerance which involves the body's immune system. The immune system overreacts to the allergen which it sees as a threat, and makes antibodies. These trigger the release of chemicals which cause the allergic reaction. Common allergens include milk, eggs, wheat, nuts, coffee, tea, fish and shellfish and food additives.

Allergies can run in families and many people react to more than one type of food. There are different theories as to what causes them. Some people believe that the use of antibiotics and additives in processed foods is causing more allergies. Recent studies estimate that one in ten children is sensitive to food additives like colours, which produce symptoms of hyperactivity. There is also evidence that giving babies and very young children certain foods can trigger allergies. Experts believe that a baby's digestive system may not be developed enough to cope with certain foods. Common allergens like cow's milk, eggs and wheat should be avoided until a child is at least six months old.

The symptoms of allergies vary in severity and in the time they take to appear. Some, such as eczema or asthma, can be delayed, then last anything from a few hours to several days. Others can be sudden and violent. The throat and tongue swell, the

Parents are advised to avoid certain foods which can trigger allergies in young babies.

heart rate rises and blood pressure drops, leading to collapse and in severe cases, death. This is called anaphylactic shock. Peanut allergy is an anaphylactic food allergy. It can develop within a few seconds or minutes of eating peanuts and is the leading cause of food allergy in the United States. Shellfish and fish can also lead to anaphylactic shock, although in many cases they cause mild reactions such as skin rashes.

Coeliac disease is an allergy to the protein gluten, which is found in wheat, barley, rye and oats. It affects one in 2000 children and if not managed properly can cause poor growth and weight loss. The only way to control the disease is to have a gluten-free diet. Other people are allergic to wholegrain wheat, including wheat starch. They suffer symptoms such as asthma, itchy skin and diarrhoea.

ADDITIVES

Many common additives have been linked with food intolerance. Additives are chemicals added to our food. They can be natural or manmade substances. There are around 4000 additives and in the UK the food industry uses over 200,000 tonnes of them every year. Additives have a long history. Woodsmoke, vinegar and salt have been used for centuries to preserve food. In the eighteenth century, anything from brick dust and sand to ground-up bones could be added to colour or bulk out food. Today, the use of additives is controlled by law. Rules vary in different countries. The European Union has regulated many additives and identified them with E numbers, which must be listed as ingredients on packaging.

Many shoppers now read the labels to check for additives which can cause allergies, especially in children.

> **We may consume as many as 20 different chemical additives at one sitting.**
> Jennifer Meek, *Sick Earth Syndrome and How to Survive It*

> **The food industry argues that many additives have a useful role. By preserving food, they enable bulk distribution and lengthen shelf life, keeping the cost of food down. They also help prevent food poisoning.**

Most additives are used to make food look or taste more attractive. They are also used to make food easier to process, pack or store. They include:

preservatives
to keep food safe to eat for longer. Some work by stopping the enzymes (protein substances) in food from breaking down and spoiling the food. Others prevent bacteria or moulds growing.

colourings
to restore colour lost from food during processing and make foods look "brighter". As well as natural colourings from foods like beetroot and grape skins, there are 20 artificial colours.

flavour enhancers and sweeteners
to make flavours stronger or sweeter.

emulsifiers and stabilisers
to mix oil and water together and stop them separating in foods like spreads.

antioxidants
to stop fats, oils and fat-soluble vitamins from reacting with oxygen and going rancid.

processing aids
to stop food going lumpy or sticky during processing.

Some foods, such as low-fat spreads and low-sugar drinks, would not exist without additives. But many people are concerned that we don't know enough about the long-term or cumulative effects on health of eating additives. In the UK we eat an average of 5 kg of additives every year. Over 100 E numbers have been identified as potentially harmful. Food colours like Sunset Yellow (E110), Annato (E160b) and Tartrazine (E102) which are used in products like fishfingers, cakes and soft drinks, were banned in Norway and Finland after studies linked them to hyperactivity in children, and to migraines and asthma. Benzoates (E210 219) which are common preservatives, have been linked with skin conditions, asthma, migraine and hyperactivity.

> **Some people argue that many food additives are unnecessary and are for the benefit of food producers rather than consumers.**

There is concern that some additives may even be used to bulk out or disguise second-rate foods, such as fatty meat products. Unwrapped foods, such as sweets, breads and cakes, often carry no information on additives. Additives used in fast food and takeaways and in restaurant meals are undeclared. Even in labelled foods, additives that have been mixed with other additives or ingredients before use in the final product do not have to be declared.

Not all foods are labelled to show the additives they contain.

> **The sad truth is that most customers not only want convenience foods but want them to appear 'fresh', 'healthy' and 'appealing'. And that is an impossible combination without additives.**
>
> Reay Tannahill, *Food in History*

DIAGNOSIS AND TREATMENT

Diagnosing food intolerance is one of the most difficult areas in medicine. Doctors may refer patients to a dietitian or specialist allergy clinic. Four main detection methods are used.

- keeping a detailed food diary and recording any unpleasant symptoms

- avoiding a suspect food for a prescribed number of weeks to see if symptoms remain.

- a skin prick test which uses injections of tiny quantities of liquid extracts of suspect foods. The skin will react to allergens.

- a Rast or radioallergosorbent test which uses a blood sample to measure levels of antibodies in the blood.

Some experts believe that the only reliable method is to eliminate suspect foods, then if there is improvement, carry out a 'blind challenge'. A detailed diet history is taken, then the patient follows a recommended diet excluding the suspect food, for two to three weeks. If the symptoms improve, the suspect food is gradually reintroduced. The test can be confirmed by giving the food in disguise to see if symptoms recur. The patient then follows a recommended diet, which is nutritionally balanced but excludes the food allergen.

Some new treatments are more controversial. Neutralisation involves injecting dilutions of the allergen into a patient. If patients show a positive allergic reaction, their symptoms can be neutralised by giving a weaker dilution or 'neutralising' dose. Once identified, this can be used at home as a drop on the tongue.

EPD or Enzyme Potentiated Desensitisation uses an enzyme called betaglucoronidase to desensitize an allergen. The patient's skin is scratched and the enzyme plus food extract is applied so it is absorbed. This treatment has proved effective in some hyperactive children but is still controversial.

Question
The food industry claims that shoppers 'prefer colourful products'. How much do you think the look of food matters?

Find out!
Which additives are used in some of your favourite processed foods? Do you think they are all necessary?

WHAT IS FOOD POISONING?

Food poisoning is any disease caused by eating food or drinking water contaminated by bacteria, toxins or viruses. Food can also be unsafe because of accidental contamination by chemicals, metals or radioactivity. Occasionally, a batch of food is deliberately contaminated with chemicals, or fragments of glass or metal, usually as a criminal means of protest. The symptoms of food poisoning include vomiting, diarrhoea, headache and aching joints. Severe cases, in high risk groups like babies, pregnant women and the sick or elderly, can lead to death.

Modern bulk food production involves many stages 'from farm to table'. Hygiene has to be a priority to avoid contamination.

> **In recent years, cases of food poisoning in the UK have increased five-fold. A 1994 survey found that food poisoning cost the UK economy £1 billion a year in lost production, absenteeism and health service costs. In the US, 6.5 million cases of food poisoning are recorded each year.**

Food poisoning is not a new phenomenon. In medieval times, there were widespread outbreaks of food poisoning caused by a mould called ergot, found in rye bread. Today, as the food chain has grown longer, the number of people likely to be affected by an outbreak of food poisoning has grown larger. Food can be contaminated at any point from production on the farm or in the sea, through factory processing, display and retail in shops, to preparation and consumption at home.

Our bodies have natural defences to break down and eliminate many toxins. Eating a varied diet also helps ensure we don't consume toxins in dangerously high quantities. Some foods, however, contain natural toxins which cause food poisoning, such as oxalic acid in rhubarb leaves and solanine in green and sprouting potatoes. Shellfish can be contaminated by toxins from the algae that they eat, and some forms of fungi are highly toxic. In some cases, toxins can be destroyed by careful preparation and cooking. Red kidney beans need to be soaked then boiled in fresh water for at least 20 minutes to remove powerful toxins called lectins. Some types of cassava need to be peeled, soaked, grated and dried to remove the toxins which can lead to nerve damage and death.

All foods deteriorate and decay in time, due to the action of bacteria. Most of the microorganisms that live in the air, in foods and on our bodies, are harmless, and some are used to make foods like yogurt, cheese and bread. But some microorganisms, including bacteria, yeasts, moulds and viruses, can multiply in food and drink, and cause food poisoning if consumed. Mouldy apples contain a toxin called patulin, and nuts and grains can be contaminated by dangerous mycotoxins called aflatoxins, which can cause liver damage and cancer. The most common food poisoning bacteria include salmonella, campylobacter and listeria monocytogenes.

Mouldy apples can contain a dangerous toxin.

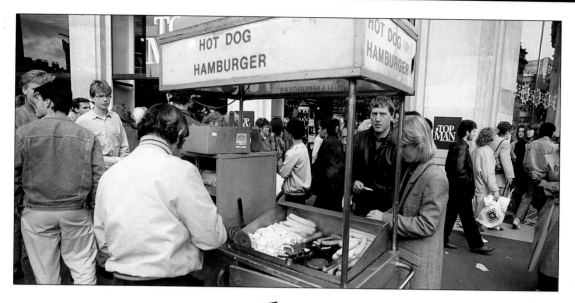

Food inspectors must check every kind of food outlet for food safety. Mobile food stalls can carry extra risks in food preparation, handling, and storage.

FOOD SAFETY LAWS

Most countries have legislation to help ensure food safety. Industrialised countries have well developed systems but in some developing countries, systems for food inspection, monitoring and testing may be inadequate. International safety standards are set by the Codex Alimentarius Commission, or Food Code, founded in 1963 and jointly run by the Food and Agriculture Organisation and the World Health Organisation. Food code committees specialise in issues like food hygiene and pesticide residues, issuing recommendations and codes of practice. It is then up to individual governments to turn these into law.

In the UK, a series of food scares in the 1980s led to the Food Safety Act 1990, followed by new regulations to meet the European Union's Food Hygiene Directive. The Food Act introduced stricter laws for all food businesses including compulsory cool storage for many foods, and Use By dates for perishable foods. Under the law, environmental health officers and trading standards officers have powers to carry out inspections. They can issue improvement notices, or if there is a threat to public health, close premises down. In the event of a food emergency, central government may issue a Food and Environment Protection Act order, to prevent the distribution and sale of contaminated foods. The law covers every kind of food business, from vending machines and hot dog vans to five star restaurants and hotels. It requires businesses to use controls such as buying from reputable suppliers, rotating stock, storing food at correct temperatures and training staff in food safety and hygiene.

FOOD-BORNE DISEASES

In developing countries, the biggest threat to food safety is contaminated water. Cholera, dysentery, typhoid, TB and Hepatitis A are all caused by dirty water. In places where water is scarce, the same source may be used for washing people and animals, swimming, cooking and washing clothes and dishes. In parts of South America, the Middle East, Africa and Asia, sanitation may be primitive, increasing the risk of contamination by sewage. Many families live in crowded conditions with no running water, no refrigerator and only wood fires for cooking. Parasites, flies, cockroaches and rodents can all contaminate food in storage. In hot climates, bacteria multiply rapidly. Food technology such as irradiation for perishable foods and sterilisation or ultra-heat treatment for milk is used to lengthen storage times. Tourists travelling to countries where food or water may be contaminated are advised to boil or sterilise water or used bottled water and drinks, and avoid foods such as salads, unpeeled fruit, shellfish and ice cream.

FROM FARM TO TABLE

In the industrialised world, food poisoning is increasing in spite of tighter regulations controlling production, processing and retailing. Some people see it as the price we have to pay for a convenient, centralised food system. Others believe it reflects major problems in the way food has been produced

and eaten since the Second World War. Modern livestock are more susceptible to infection than traditional breeds because they have been selected for growth potential rather than disease resistance. Foodstuffs containing animal protein to sustain productivity may be contaminated with salmonella and other bacteria. Infections can spread easily in the crowded and stressed environment of intensive units and in abbatoirs.

Battery egg production can increase the risk of salmonella.

> ❝ **Fifty to sixty per cent of poultry and their eggs in the UK are infected with salmonella.** ❞

After the BSE crisis, the UK government set up the Meat Hygiene Service to ensure standards of hygiene in abattoirs.

> ❝ **There needs to be a sea change in the way we look at agriculture policy in this country... There has been a revolution in consumer attitudes, post-BSE, and food safety and quality has come into it now, not just protection of the environment.** ❞
>
> *Patrick Holden, Director of the Soil Association*

Some outbreaks of food poisoning are due to changes in the methods of preparation and storage of foods. The central production of meals for mass-catering outlets such as airlines, schools and hospitals has led to development of methods like cook-chill,

cook-freeze and sous-vide. Meals are prepared and cooked in advance, then chilled or frozen, and later reheated. Problems arise when food is stored at insufficiently low temperatures, or is inadequately cooked or reheated. Cook-chill foods, for example, should be stored at 8°C or below, but five types of food poisoning bacteria, including listeria and E coli, can multiply at temperatures between 5° and 8°C.

Most foods we buy today are plastic-wrapped. This keeps out microorganisms in the air, but there is scientific evidence that chemicals called phthalates can migrate into food through the wrapping. These act like the female hormone oestrogen and can cause fertility problems and cancer. Current advice is to avoid film wrap on fatty foods and in the microwave. There is also concern that vacuum packing, used for foods like meat products, cheese and coffee, can encourage the growth of the rare but dangerous clostridium botulinum bacterium. Scientists are continuing research into the safety of food packaging.

FOOD HYGIENE

At the end of the food chain, responsibility for food safety lies with the consumer. At temperatures between 15° and 35°C, with food and moisture, bacteria can multiply rapidly. They become dormant at very cold temperatures, so meat and other perishable foods need careful storage in refrigerators, under 5°C .

Hygiene is obviously important at all stages of food handling.

Food hygiene rules include:

- checking refrigerator temperatures daily

- storing raw and cooked foods separately

- always following Use By dates

- keeping kitchen surfaces and utensils spotless

- washing hands before preparing or eating food

- avoiding cross contamination of foods, by washing chopping boards and knives used for meat and poultry before re-use.

- covering any cuts or grazes when preparing food

- never coughing or sneezing over food

- cooking foods thoroughly, especially meat and poultry

- reheating foods thoroughly, once only

- keeping animals, flies and other pests out of the kitchen

> " Is the consumer responsible for adequate cooking to kill off the effects of poor hygiene practices during production, or is the processor or retailer responsible for providing uncontaminated food? "
>
> Geoff Tansey and Tony Worsley in *The Food System*

Find out!
What food safety policies do your nearest major supermarkets have?

Question
Who do you think is responsible for food safety: producers or consumers?

As reported cases of food poisoning go on rising, people are still debating where the primary responsibility for food safety lies. Some people believe that major changes in the modern food system are required. In 1997, the UK government announced plans for the creation of a new Food and Countryside Ministry to replace MAFF and a new Food Standards Agency to report to the secretary of state for health.

DO WE NEED INTENSIVE FARMING?

In the last 50 years, intensive methods of farming have enabled a vast increase in food production. Farms have grown larger and more specialised, with animals herded into intensive indoor units. Hedges have been dug out to enlarge fields, enabling the use of large farm machinery and cutting labour costs. Crop yields have been boosted by selective breeding, chemical fertilisers and pesticides.

Animals have been changed by selective breeding and high protein feeds to grow and fatten faster, producing more meat, eggs and milk. Foods like chicken and turkey, which used to be eaten only occasionally, have become cheap, popular everyday meals.

Some people argue that intensive methods are necessary to feed the demands of a growing population for a varied and nutritious diet. Others are concerned about the effects of intensive farming on human health, animal welfare and the environment.

"Monoculture" farming aims for maximum productivity.

> 66 **A field of wheat now produces two and a half times as much grain as in 1945.** 99

FACTORY FARMING

Most poultry, pigs and calves on modern farms are kept indoors in intensive units. Some people argue that intensive units enable farmers to keep a close check on livestock. They claim that indoor units keep animals warm and dry and protect them from predators and diseases. There is now, however, increasing evidence that intensive methods breed infections, as well as problems like brittle bones, lameness, heart disease and stress.

Intensively reared animals live only a few weeks of their natural lifespan because selective breeding, a high protein diet and growth-promoting hormones have speeded up their growth rate. Chickens have reached twice their natural weight when they are killed for the table at seven weeks old. Some people are concerned that the routine use of antibiotics is allowing antibiotic-resistant bacteria to enter the food chain. There is also concern about the use of growth-promoting hormones, although these have been banned within the European Union.

Poultry farmers refer to 'crops' of chicks.

Question
Would your family be willing to pay more for humanely reared meat?

THE BSE CRISIS

The emergence of Bovine Spongiform Encephalopathy or 'Mad Cow' disease in the late 1980s focussed attention on animal feed and welfare under intensive systems. Vegetarian animals such as cattle and sheep have been turned into meat-eaters by the use of high protein feeds containing waste bones, meat and offal. In the late 1970s, there were changes in the regulations controlling the meat rendering industry. Government scientists believe that this allowed Scrapie, a brain disease found in sheep, to enter the food chain in sheep meat and bonemeal fed to cattle. Another theory is that organophosphate pesticides, used to control warble fly in cattle, may have entered the animals' nervous systems, deforming the prion protein which is believed to cause BSE. Working on the advice of government scientists, the use of sheep and cattle protein in animal feedstuffs was banned in 1988. The following year MAFF banned the use of beef brains and offal in human foodstuffs. The number of confirmed cases of BSE rose from 2000 in 1988 to over 34,000 in 1993, increasing concern over possible links between BSE and the human brain disease CJD, or CreutzfeldtJakob disease.

The European Union banned exports of British beef, and 2 million cows were slaughtered under a European Union compensation scheme. In 1997, scientists in London and Edinburgh confirmed that their research showed that a new variant of CJD had migrated to humans from eating BSE-infected meat. Later in the year, acting on scientific evidence, the government banned the sale of beef on the bone. CJD is known to have a long incubation period, making the numbers infected impossible to calculate. BSE has had a devastating effect on the British beef industry, and on consumer confidence in food safety.

CHEMICAL PESTICIDES AND FERTILISERS

Nitrogen fertilisers have vastly increased food production since the Second World War. Recently, however, concern has grown over levels of nitrates found in our food and water. When we take in nitrates, bacteria in our digestive systems can reduce them to nitrites, and these in turn can form compounds which are known to cause cancer.

Pesticides are chemicals used by farmers to control pests, diseases and weeds. In the past 30 years, pesticide sales worldwide have increased 31 times. Many people are worried about the long-term effects of pesticides on human health and the environment. Pesticide chemicals are highly toxic and in excessive doses can attack the nervous system, damage DNA and cause cancer and birth defects. Pesticide residues have been found in Arctic snow, underground wells and rivers and in human body tissue and breast milk.

> **In effect, we have been part of a vast unplanned experiment into the capacity of the biosphere and its inhabitatants to withstand attack by chemicals designed to destroy living tissue and injure reproductive and nervous systems.**
>
> David Nicholson-Lord, *The Independent*, 1993

The use of pesticides is controlled by laws. The World Health Organisation has calculated Acceptable Daily Intakes (ADIs) which is the amount of a chemical which can be consumed every day in a lifetime with a 'practical certainty of no harm'. From the ADIs, permitted Maximum Residue Levels or MRLs are set.

Pesticide residues arise either from legal use before or after harvest, or from illegal use. Chemicals can be misused by applying too much, or too frequently, or too close to harvest. A 1995 report found that nearly half

A farmer spraying winter wheat. Do we need to use so many chemicals?

of produce tested contained residues, two per cent above the MRLs. Some showed traces of banned chemicals, either from illegal use in the UK or on imports from countries where those pesticides were still in use. Since then, residues exceeding safety recommendations have been found on milk and dairy products, vegetables and fruit.

There is much debate over 'safe levels' of pesticide residue. One US toxicologist has produced calculations suggesting that we consume 1.5 grams of natural toxins a day in foods like coffee, wheat, rice and potatoes, about 10,000 times the average amount of pesticide residues consumed. Others point out that pesticides are artificial and our bodies have not had thousands of years to adapt to them as they have to natural toxins. According to Greenpeace, consumers in northern Europe take in more than 40 different pesticide residues in food and drink every day. Little is known about the 'mixing bowl' effect of eating a variety of residues over a long period. Some experts believe they are responsible for rising cancer rates, reductions in male fertility and the growth of allergy-related diseases.

Some people argue that pesticides are necessary to control pests, which still destroy 30 per cent of world agriculture, to keep costs down and to provide attractive, blemish-free foods for consumers. But others argue for less chemically intensive methods. They point out that the number of insect species that have become resistant to pesticides has increased from 12 in 1946 to 829 in the 1980s. Pesticides also kill natural predators which could be used to control pests. New research shows that farmers would benefit financially from using less pesticides.

FOOD SURPLUSES

Many people question why we need intensive farming when many developed countries are already producing too much food. In the European Union, the Common Agricultural Policy (CAP) has encouraged farmers to produce as much as possible without regard for long-term environmental concerns. If prices of major commodities fall below a certain level, government agencies buy up surpluses and put them in store, creating grain and butter mountains, and wine and olive oil lakes. Quotas on production have been introduced for products like milk, and farmers are given subsidies to set aside land to reduce surpluses.

> **I have a dream.** Instead of government paying the farmers to keep land out of production because of the creation of huge mountains of surplus foodstuffs by the use of intensive farming methods, my dream is that it will subsidize the farmers to return this nonproductive land to use organically.
>
> Jean Boht, Parents for Safe Food

ORGANIC FARMING

Concern for the environment and for animal welfare, and the desire to produce and eat healthy foods, has led to a renewed interest in organic farming. Organic farmers combine traditional methods such as enriching the soil with manure and rotating crops, with modern soil science, crop breeding and ecology. Organic farming needs more manpower and crops may have lower yields but research shows that productivity does not fall dramatically when farms convert to organic methods. Natural predators can be introduced to control pests, and organic foods should be free of pesticide residues, although they can be affected by spray drift from conventional farms. The benefits of organic farming include reduction in air and water pollution, preservation of natural habitats, and higher standards of animal welfare. Animals are kept free range and are not given routine antibiotics or growth hormones or food stuffs containing animal protein. Some people say that organic farming can never produce enough food to replace conventional methods, but others argue that a change in government subsidies could expand the market. At present, MAFF spends more in monitoring pesticide residues (£2 million a year) than it does on researching and supporting organic farming. Organic produce is more expensive to buy, but the market is growing, reflecting consumers' concerns.

> " There is no doubt that over the last few years, a growing anxiety has developed amongst all sections of the community about the consequences of modern, intensive farming methods. It is increasingly felt by members of the public that large scale soil erosion, the destruction of wildlife habitats, and the excessive use of chemicals and unnatural substances are unacceptable and cannot continue unabated without ruining the countryside for future generations and probably causing long-term health hazards. "
>
> Prince Charles,
> British Organic Farmers Conference, 1989

Find Out

How much organic produce does your nearest supermarket stock? How does this compare with five years ago?

HOW IS SCIENCE CHANGING OUR FOOD?

Farmers and plant breeders have been changing the food we eat for hundreds of years. They have improved crops and animals by selecting the best examples to breed the next generation. They have produced new cross breeds, giving stronger, faster-growing animals and crops with higher yields. But selective breeding can be slow and uncertain. Science now offers faster and more precise ways of changing crops and animals through genetic engineering.

places, then insert new segments and stitch the strand back together. Gene splicing allows new varieties to be created with great precision. Food scientists can create crops that are pest resistant or can tolerate frost, drought or poor soils. They can also design foods, such as potatoes which are ideal for crisp making, or wheat for bread making.

Much of the food we eat today is designed in food laboratories.

> **" The objective behind genetic manipulation is not better foodstuffs, but generally quicker, cheaper production in greater volumes. "**
> Dagmar Roth Behrendt, Reporter to the European Parliament

Living organisms have thousands of units of heredity called genes which determine their characteristics. Scientists can now select individual genes and move them from one organism to another, to breed in features like fast growth or disease resistance. They use enzymes to break the DNA strands in certain

In the US alone, some 370 field tests into genetically engineered foods are in progress. Genetically engineered tomatoes, soy beans, corn, squash and potatoes are already on the market. The first genetically engineered soy beans were harvested in 1996. The beans were injected with a gene from a bacterium which is resistant to glyphosate weed killers. This allows farmers to use glyphosate on their crops rather than more expensive selective weedkillers. Europe imports 14 million tonnes of US soya a year, and soya is used in two thirds of all supermarket foods. Consumer groups have called for segregation of genetically engineered beans to give consumers choice.

> " Living things do not exist solely for the benefit of humans. We have been around for only ten thousand years while life began four thousand million years ago. How can we usurp creation, the sanctity of life, and believe it is ours to tinker with? "
>
> Eric Brunner, Research Association, London Food Commission, 1990

> " A major commercial objective of biotechnology is to produce plants which are no longer sensitive to plant pests, drastically reducing the need for insecticide spraying. This seems to be an obvious good thing. "
>
> Dr Jonathon Jones, Sainsbury Laboratory, John Innes Institute, 1990

In Australia, they have discovered how to genetically alter coffee plants to produce caffeine-free beans. At present, coffee beans are decaffeinated by washing with chemicals, which can affect flavour and smell.

In the future, it may be possible to manufacture many foods, even meat, in the laboratory, replacing natural production. Some people argue that genetic engineering will help to feed the world's growing population. But others see it as a dangerous, short-term fix. They are concerned that biotechnology companies could effectively take control of food production, by taking out patents for genetically engineered crops and animals.

Question

Do you think it would be right to grow meat in the laboratory?

FOR AND AGAINST

These are some of the arguments in favour of genetic engineering:

For
Crops can be given a gene to protect them from pests, so reducing the need for chemical pesticides.

For
Perishable foods like fruit can be altered to ripen slowly, giving them longer shelf life and saving on wastage.

For
Crops can be developed to tolerate conditions like drought and frost, increasing productivity.

For
Food scientists can create foods to meet consumer needs.

These are some of the arguments against genetic engineering:

Against
Only two per cent of foods are altered to improve taste or nutrition. The remaining 98 per cent are altered to speed up food production and processing by the major food companies.

Against
There is a risk that genetically altered plants and animals will be stronger and may threaten the survival of other species, reducing biodiversity.

Against
There is a risk that toxic substances and allergens could be transferred from one food to another. Soy beans, injected with a gene from brazil nuts, caused allergic reactions in people with nut allergies. Genes could also pass on antibiotic resistance to humans.

Against
Self-protecting genes could transfer to weeds, creating a new breed of superweeds. Viruses could be stimulated to mutate into stronger forms which could attack other species.

TRANSGENIC FOOD

Scientists are now able to move genetic material across species barriers, inserting human genes into animals, or fish genes into plants, to breed in new features. Genes from the flounder, a type of flatfish which contains antifreeze proteins to protect its cells, have been transferred to tomatoes and potatoes to make them frost-resistant. In the future,

Perishable foods may be genetically modified or irradiated.

foods could contain material from hundreds of unrelated species of animals, insects, bacteria and plants. Many people believe that mixing genetic material is dangerous and unethical. Vegetarians, for example, might be eating plant foods which contain animal genes.

Question

"This is imperfect technology with inherent dangers... It is the unpredictability of the outcomes that is the most worrying." Should we change the genetic makeup of animals reared for food?

DOLLY THE SHEEP

In 1995 scientists introduced Dolly, the world's first cloned sheep. They had taken cells from a donor sheep and grown them in the laboratory, then inserted them into an unfertilised egg from another sheep, which had had its nucleus, containing genetic information, removed. The egg was then placed inside a surrogate mother sheep. The technique of cloning could significantly speed up selective breeding, and there are predictions that within two years, 85 per cent of British cattle could be cloned, but many people oppose cloning on ethical grounds and there are concerns that genetic weaknesses could spread more quickly.

Animals are also being genetically altered to grow larger and increase yields. Dairy cattle injected with the growth hormone bovine somatotropin (BST) which can be manufactured in the laboratory by genetic engineering, can increase their milk yields by up to a fifth, but there is evidence that cows may become sick more often, requiring more antibiotics. A 1995 report by Compassion in World Farming found increased abortion rates in sheep injected with genetically engineered hormones to make them self-shearing, and chickens, genetically altered to have greater salmonella resistance, suffered higher cancer rates.

NUTRICEUTICALS

Food scientists are now designing foods to enhance the body's immune system, prevent disease and delay ageing. In the US, chicken feed has been altered to produce eggs with less fat and cholesterol and three times the vitamin E. The US National Cancer Institute is currently spending $20 million on developing anticancer foods using compounds from fruit and vegetables. In the UK, scientists have crossed broccoli with a species of wild cabbage to increase levels of a substance called sulphurophane. This backs up the body's natural defences by turning on special enzymes which mop up cancer-causing agents. They have also identified a variety of rye grass which is unusually high in linolenic acid, a fat which can reduce cholesterol in the blood. This could be used to produce low cholesterol milk and beef.

> **66** In future, it will be possible to design foods with built-in medicines. Some people see nutriceuticals as a new generation of health foods. Others believe there are risks in interfering with the natural balance of foods and our bodies. **99**

Question
Would you eat food that had been modified to contain medicine?

IRRADIATION

Irradiation was first used in 1916 in experiments on strawberries in Sweden. At irradiation plants, foods are packaged and pretreated by refrigeration or heating before being bombarded with electrons or with gamma rays from radioactive material. Provided it is properly controlled, irradiation does not make food radioactive but it does produce chemical changes. In low doses, it inhibits the sprouting of vegetables, delays ripening and kills insect pests. Medium doses can reduce microorganisms like yeasts, moulds and bacteria to extend the shelf life of food and reduce risk of food poisoning. High doses sterilise food, killing all bacteria and viruses.

> **66** It should be readily apparent that this is a 'hightech' attempt to paper over the rapidly widening cracks of our modern food production techniques. Food irradiation marks the zenith of misguided technical 'fixes' for problems that have to be tackled at source, via a bold and possibly radical reappraisal of the way we produce, handle and distribute our food. **99**
>
> Sir Julian Rose, *The Times*, 1990

Laws controlling irradiation vary in different countries. In Russia, it is used to preserve the grain crop, and in many European countries it is used to sterilise spices and herbs. In the UK, irradiation became a legal means of processing food under the Food Safety Act of 1990. Irradiated foods must be labelled, unless they make up less than a quarter of a compound ingredient. The majority of irradiated foods are used in processed foods. Some people argue that irradiation will help improve the quality of food and reduce cases of food poisoning. Others see it as a 'quick fix' solution.

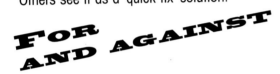

These are some of the arguments in favour of irradiation:

For
It may help prevent food poisoning, especially in hot countries where fresh foods spoil quickly.

For
By extending shelf life, it will make storage and distribution easier and reduce wastage of food.

For
It may reduce the need for some chemical preservatives.

For
It may improve the taste and texture of certain foods.

For
It could help in food processing, such as improving the elasticity of dough in breadmaking.

These are some of the arguments against irradiation:

Against
Between 20 and 80 per cent of vitamins and some essential fatty acids can be lost. Vitamin E is almost completely destroyed.

Against
Irradiated food looks fresh but although bacteria are reduced, the chemical toxins they may have made earlier are still present.

Against
There is a risk that irradiation could cause viruses, insects or bacteria in food to mutate, leading to more resistant strains.

Against
Chemical additives may be needed to offset some undesirable effects, such as discoloration or the breakdown of fats in meat.

Against
We don't know whether there could be long-term effects on human health.

Many people argue that all irradiated foods should be fully labelled. They are concerned that unscrupulous producers could use irradiation to conceal contaminated food.

As scientists continue to change the way our food is produced and processed, the arguments surrounding the use of biotechnology in food production are sure to increase.

Question
You have read the arguments for and against irradiation. Where do you stand on this issue and why?

HELPLINES

The British Dietetic Association
Elisabeth House
22 Suffolk Street Queensway
Birmingham B1 1LS
Tel: 0121 643 5483

British Nutrition Foundation
52-54 High Holborn
London WC1V 6RQ
Tel: 0171 404 6504
Information and advice on
nutrition and health related
matters

British Heart Foundation
14 Fitzhardinge Street
London W1H 4DH
Tel: 0171 935 0185
Information and advice on
healthy eating

Foodsense
Mass Publications
London SE99 7TP
Tel: 0645 556000
Leaflets on aspects of UK
government food policy

Eating Disorders Association
1st floor Wensum House
103 Prince of Wales Road
Norwich Norfolk NR1 1DW
Tel: 01603 619090
Youth Helpline: 01603 765050
Leaflets, booklets, telephone
helplines, national network of
self-help groups

The National Centre for Eating Disorders
54 New Road Esher
Surrey KT10 9NU
Tel: 01372 469493
Information pack and personal
assessments, personal, postal
and telephone programmes, day
workshops

The Vegetarian Society
Parkdale Dunham Road
Altrincham Cheshire WAI4 4QG
Tel: 0161 928 0793
Books, leaflets, information on
vegetarianism

Food Additives Campaign Team
Science Policy Unit
Mantall Building University of
Sussex Brighton BN1 9RF
Tel: 01273 686 758

Ministry of Agriculture, Food and Fisheries
Food Safety Directorate
Nobel House 17 Smith Square
London SW1P 3HX
Helpline: 0645 335577

Food Safety Advisory Centre
Foodline 14 Soho Square
London W1V 5FB
Foodline: 0800 282407
Information on food safety

The Soil Association
Bristol House 40-56 Victoria
Street Bristol BS1 6BY
Tel: 0117 929 0661
Information on organic foods
and farming

The Pesticides Trust
Eurolink Centre 49 Effra Road
London SW2 1BZ
Tel: 0171 274 8895
Information on the health,
environmental and policy
aspects of pesticides

The Food Commission
3rd floor 5-11 Worship Street
London EC2A 2BH
Tel: 0171 837 2250
Publishes *The Food Magazine*
and books dealing with a wide
range of food issues

AUSTRALIA AND NEW ZEALAND

Australian Consumers Association
452 Flinders Street
Melbourne Vic. 3000
Tel: (03) 9627 6000

Australian Nutrition Foundation
260 Kooyong Road
Caulfield Vic 3162
Tel: (03) 9528 2453

Australian Food Industry Science Centre
Sneydes Road
Werribee Vic 3030
Tel: (03) 9742 0111

FURTHER READING

Food and Nutrition Anita Tull, Oxford University Press 1996
Comprehensive paperback on food and nutrition

Forbidden Body: Why being fat is not a sin Shelley Bovey, Pandora 1994
The author sets out to uncover the prejudice against fat women

The Beauty Myth Naomi Wolf, Chatto and Windus 1990
Study exposing the lies behind the cult of female beauty

Never Diet Again Kano, Thorsons 1990
Practical guide on how to achieve freedom from a weight/dieting obsession

National Dairy Council Nutrition Service Factfiles:
Series of pamphlets on food and nutrition

Beyond Chaotic Eating A way out of Anorexia, Bulimia and Compulsive Eating Helena Wilkinson, Marshall Pickering 1993
Book written by an ex-sufferer and counsellor, giving a direct account of the part families play in the build up to an eating disorder

Talking about Anorexia How to cope with life without starving Maroushka Monro, Sheldon Press 1996
Practical book written by a recovered anorexic and ex-magazine agony aunt

Surviving an Eating Disorder Strategies for Family and Friends Siegel, Brisman and Weinshal, Harper & Row 1989
Guidelines for sufferers and friends, with practical suggestions

The Teenage Vegetarian Survival Guide Annouchka Grose, Red Fox 1992
Covers everything you need to know from what you can eat in McDonalds to how to say 'No meat please' in Turkish

Food Allergy and Intolerance Jonathan Brostoff, Bloomsbury 1993
Expert's guide to the problem of food intolerance and allergies

The New E for Additives Maurice Hanssen, Thorsons 1987
Guide to food additives and their E numbers

Unfit for Human Consumption Richard Lacey, Souvenir Press 1991
Study into the crisis surrounding the modern food industry

The Bio-revolution Cornucopia or Pandora's Box? Peter Wheale, Pluto Press 1990
Investigation into the implications of genetic engineering for people, animals, plants and the environment

Genetic Engineering: Dreams and Nightmares Enzo Russo, W.H. Freeman 1995
Account of the various applications of genetic engineering and the impact it has made

Irradiation: the Facts Tony Webb and Dr Tim Land, London Food Commission 1987
Investigation into the science and effects of food irradiation

INDEX

Additives 7, 36, 37-9, 40
Agriculture
    Common Agricultural
    Policy (CAP) 51
    in developing countries 14
    early civilisations 8
    intensive farming 47-52
    organic farming 52
    pesticides 43, 49-51
    see also Livestock
Allergies see Food
    intolerance/allergies
Animal welfare 7, 32-3, 34
    see also Livestock
Anorexia nervosa 26, 27

Binge eating disorder 27
BSE (Bovine Spongiform
    Encephalopathy) 30, 45,
    49
Bulimia nervosa 27

Calories 10
    and slimming diets 22, 24
Cancer
    and diet 15-17, 30, 31
    and nutriceuticals 57
    and pesticides 49, 51
Carbohydrates 9, 10, 15
    and slimming diets 22, 24
Cash crops 14
Children
    and eating disorders 25-6
    food habits 7

hyperactivity in 38
and obesity 18
and physical activity 19
and slimming diets 21, 24
Cholesterol 16, 57
CJD (CreutzfeldtJakob
    disease) 49

Diet 7, 8-14
    balanced 9-11, 22
    effects on health 15-20
    in history 8
    slimming diets 8, 21-4
Diet-related diseases 14,
    15-17

E numbers 37, 38
E-coli bacteria 30, 45
Eating disorders 25-8
Egg production, and
    salmonella 44-5
Environmental issues 33-4
EPD (Enzyme Potentiated
    Desensitisation) 40
European Union
    and the BSE crisis 49
    Common Agricultural
    Policy (CAP) 51
    and factory farming 48
    Food Hygiene Directive 43
Exercise see also Physical
    activity

F Plan diet 23

Factory farming 34, 44, 48-9
Fair trade 14
Families
    and eating disorders 25,
        26, 28
    eating habits 12
Farming see Agriculture;
    Livestock
Fashion models 21-2
Fast foods 11, 12, 39
Fat consumption 9, 11, 16,
    30
Food combining diets 23
Food diaries 28, 40
Food hygiene 43, 45-6
Food intolerance/allergies
    35-40
    and additives 36, 37-9,
        40
    diagnosis and treatment
        40
    symptoms of 36-7
    triggers 35
Food packaging 45
Food poisoning 30, 38, 41-6
    costs to the economy 41
    and irradiation 58
    symptoms 41
    and toxins 42
Food Safety Act (1990) 43,
    58
Food safety laws 7, 43, 46
Food scares 7
Food storage 45

Genetic engineering 7, 53-8
Growth-promoting hormones 48

Hay diet 23
Health and diet 11, 15-20, 30-1
Heart disease, and diet 15, 16, 17, 30
Hyperactivity 38

Importing fresh fruit and vegetables 9, 13
Intensive farming 47-52
Irradiation of food 7, 44, 57-8

Japanese diet 16-17
Junk foods 19

Kilocalories *see* Calories

Listeria 42, 45
Livestock
    and BSE 30, 45, 49
    cloning 56
    factory farming 44, 47, 48-9
    and genetic engineering 53
    markets 32
    and organic farming 52
    slaughter of 32-3, 45

Local education authorities, healthy eating policies 11
Low-fat diets 8, 22, 23, 24

'Mad Cow' disease *see* BSE
Malnutrition 19-20
Meat
    consumption 30-1, 32
    laboratory manufacture of 55
Mediterranean diet 15-16
Minerals in food 9

Nutriceuticals 57
Nutrition 9-11, 29-30

Obesity 14, 17-19, 22
Organic farming 52

Packaging of food 45
Pesticides 43, 49-51
    and organic farming 52
Physical activity 7, 10, 18-19, 23
Pregnancy, diet in 9
Processed food 12, 20, 40
Proteins 9
    and vegetarian diets 29, 30

Rationing 15
Refined foods 8

Religion, and vegetarian diets 31

Salmonella 30, 42, 44-5
Salt consumption 11
Slimming diets 8, 21-4
Slimming pills 22
Soya products, and breast cancer 16-17
Sugar
    consumption 11
    hidden in foods 20
Supermarkets 7, 12, 13, 18, 46, 52

Toxins 42, 51, 58
Transgenic food 55-6
Transport, and food miles 13

Vegans 29, 30
Vegetarian diets 8, 9, 29-34
    and animal welfare 32-3, 34
    environmental issues 33-4
    health benefits 30-1
    nutrients 29-30
    and religion 31
Vitamins 8, 9

Water
    and animal farming 33
    contamined 44